Awakened

30 days of waking up and stepping out

Awakened

30 days of waking up and stepping out

SIMCHA NATAN

simchanatan.com

fb.com/simchanatan
IG: @simchanatan

Awakened *30 days of waking up and stepping out* © Simcha Natan 2018

Cover illustration by Joe Hateley © Simcha Natan

Design and layout © HerebyDesign

Edited by Abbie Robson

For R,

My bestest, my love, my partner and my life.

You have stepped into a season of being 'awakened' to all you are and have been made to be. It is an honor, privilege and joy (when I choose it!) to serve with you, to see you fly, and to do this thing called life with you.

Contents

CONTENTS

Awakened

Introduction

$\mathcal{W}$elcome to the second part of the *Dare to Ask* journey! I'm beyond excited to walk through 30 days of being awakened to the reality of who we are made to be, following the journey of learning to dream with God again.

Through writing this devotional God really spoke to me about how He wants us fully alive, with every sense, every atom, every breath bursting with life in expression of Him. This process of waking up and being switched on is a risky yet exciting one, taking us to unexpected places with unknown vistas.

My hope and prayer for you is that you find faith to step out, encouragement to stand firm, and let every part of you be awakened to the truth of Him, your dreams, and the reality of who you're made to be.

~ Simcha x

The *Dare to Ask* project is comprised by the umbrella book *Dare to Ask*, followed by the first EP and its counterpart devotional - *Dreaming - 30 days of Dreaming with God.*

Awakened is the second part of this journey and contains a second EP, its 30 day devotional counterpart and accompanying artwork.

DAY 1

A God who does not sleep

"He will not let your foot slip—
he who watches over you will not slumber;
indeed, he who watches over Israel
will neither slumber nor sleep."
Psalm 121:3-4

They went to a place called Gethsemane, and Jesus
said to his disciples, "Sit here while I pray"… Then he
returned to his disciples and found them sleeping.
Mark 14:32, 37

Yeshua (Jesus) set an example for us in the garden of Gethsemane. Whilst everyone around Him was falling asleep, He remained awake in prayer. Peter, James & John had been asked to 'remain and watch', but even they could not keep their eyes open as their Master was facing His darkest moment.

God doesn't slumber OR sleep while watching over us. He is constantly aware, constantly watching our footing as we walk out our lives. He won't nod off; He is committed to watching over our every step. We have a sure foundation that Yeshua was simply modeling the Father in that garden.

Even more incredible, though, is the fact that since His ascension, Yeshua has remained in constant prayer, not for Himself this time, but for us!

> *'Who then is the one who condemns? No one. Christ Jesus who died—more than that, who was raised to life—is at the right hand of God and is also interceding for us.'*
> *(Romans 8:34)*

Our God is El Roi: the God who sees us, who watches us, and who does not abandon His post. We can rest assured that while we may fall asleep from time to time, we have a God who does not slumber or sleep, and an advocate in Yeshua who remains in constant intercession for us.

This devotional is all about being awake to what God is doing and seeing His plans for you. Where might God be speaking to you that you are too spiritually sleepy to hear? It could be something you know is already there and you've never stepped into, or it could even something you don't yet know. Take some time today as we start this journey to be conscious of what it might mean to be fully awake, and what you wish to learn from this month of renewed vision. Remember that God sees you and is in constant prayer for you.

Day 2

Slumber

Wake up, sleeper, rise from the dead,
and Christ will shine on you.
Ephesians 5:14

Returning the third time, he said to them, "Are you
still sleeping and resting? Enough! The hour has come.
Look, the Son of Man is delivered into the hands of
sinners. 42 Rise! Let us go! Here comes my betrayer!"

Mark 14:41-42

The difference between sleep and slumber is subtle. The two are often used synonymously, but slumber usually indicates a lighter sleep, like a doze, as opposed to the full, unconscious sleep we engage in nightly.

We spend a lot of our lives sleeping, both physically and metaphorically. Physically, we need sleep in order to rejuvenate our bodies and minds. Metaphorically, we are often 'asleep' due to our circumstances. Like the disciples in the garden of Gethsemane, we let the heaviness of situations we find ourselves in to take over, and we allow 'sleep' to overcome us, shutting us down.

In order to fully engage with what God intends for our lives, we have to fully engage with life itself. We are so often sleep-walking through life, going through our daily, monotonous grind, failing to catch the joy and never fully participating. We get caught up in the rat race, feeling the pressure of a need to provide for family, or earn enough to meet the demands on life.

This explains why so many of us don't know what we are called to or what our dreams or gifts are. We don't value ourselves or our gifts enough to invest in them. We are asleep - sometimes so much so that we have lost any awareness of our gifts at all! Unaware of ourselves and unaware of what we carry, we are switched off to the daily opportunities God gives to use our gifts and callings for His eternal purpose. Some of us have never figured out who we are, so our gifts simply fizzle away.

Today it is time to dig deep and search our hearts. Have we fallen into slumber? Have we detached ourselves from our gifts? Do we know what God has called us to? Are there areas in our lives that are 'sleeping'?

Decide today that you are committed to waking up, and ask God to shine His light on those areas that have been dozing. We are created to be fully alive, not half unconscious!

Day 3

Waking up

*My frame was not hidden from you
when I was made in the secret place,
when I was woven together in the depths of the earth.
Your eyes saw my unformed body;
all the days ordained for me were written in your
book before one of them came to be.
Psalm 139:15-16*

*And do this, understanding the present time: The
hour has already come for you to wake up from your
slumber, because our salvation is nearer now than
when we first believed.
Romans 13:11*

I've realized that the older I get, the less I know about myself, and the more there is to understand. But I've also realized that life is all about becoming more awakened to who God has made us to be and what He has put inside of us. It's about learning about how He intends for us to partner with Him.

Some of us may never have even considered that God's plan was intricately woven together in the way He created us. We may have never asked Him to open our eyes to who we are, so we remain 'asleep' to His plan. There is great delight in realizing that God did not make any mistakes when He created us. He's not lost His diary - He is always on time, and has never said "oops"! He can always bring together the creation He has made with the events He has orchestrated, at exactly the right time.

The process of waking up physically can be difficult, particularly if we have been in a deep, long sleep. We can feel nauseous, disorientated and confused. Maybe we've forgotten where we are, or how we got there. Spiritual awakening can be similar - sometimes the cost of starting to wake up to who we are and re-engaging with God's intentions is like that short period of feeling uncomfortable.

But it is always worth pushing through that short time in order to get back in touch with who we have been made to be. It is an eternally long adventure of discovery of God's creation, to truly grapple with who we are, each person created uniquely with their own gifts, talents, dreams and calling. If we fall asleep to this, those gifts may never be used for their original intention. They lie like unopened gifts, never really taken out of their packaging to be used, admired or to bless others.

Ask God to open your eyes today to see the intricacies of how He has created you uniquely. Ask Him to give you a glimpse of the purpose He formed for you in your mother's womb. Maybe there are gifts that you know are dormant, or maybe there are more gifts that you haven't discovered yet! This adventure is all about you daring to ask God to reveal those things, to awakened those sleepy gifts and finding new release in them.

DAY 4

Grogginess

So then, let us not be like others, who are asleep, but let us be awake and sober.
1 Thessalonians 5:6

In the presence of God and of Christ Jesus, who will judge the living and the dead, and in view of his appearing and his kingdom, I give you this charge: Preach the word; be prepared in season and out of season; correct, rebuke and encourage—with great patience and careful instruction.

2 Timothy 4:1-2

There are two kinds of people - morning people, and night time people. Some are able to spring out of bed at 5am ready to GO, while the rest of us can take a couple of hours to fully engage our minds and bodies to the day's tasks because we at our best later in the evening.

Kids can be particularly amusing to observe in their freshly woken up state. They are quiet, dazed, and start the day in slow motion, staring intently at something in the middle distance, unable to respond to conversation with more than a grunt.

This groggy state can be used to illustrate another scary reality: some of us may be sort of awake, and yet unable to use our voices to their capacity, or engage with the world around us. We are present physically, but unable to participate fully in all that is going on. We, too, stare intently into the 'middle distance', whether into a smart device or other mundane things. In this groggy state we are unable to utter anything meaningful to those around us, and even if words do come out their impact is limited, like that of a morning grunt.

It is possible to snap out of this groggy, dozy state. It is possible to be fully alive, fully engaged and fully intentional in how we live. We can make the choice to shake off the grogginess and fully play the role that was written for us even before we were born, making the impact that God designed us for.

Take time today to identify any areas in your life that are still in this groggy state. It may be that you've started the wake-up process, but some areas are lagging behind. Make an effort to intentionally converse with God through your day, letting nothing pass you by. Let your words be led by him, and pray that you'll always be ready to bring His blessing to those around you.

Day 5

Sudden wake up

Then the angel who talked with me returned and woke me up, like someone awakened from sleep. He asked me, "What do you see?"

I answered, "I see a solid gold lampstand with a bowl at the top and seven lamps on it, with seven channels to the lamps."

Zechariah 4:1-2

Some of us need a wake-up call, like a cold bucket of water being thrown on us to fully wake us up. God uses events around us to bring a sense of urgency, a sudden understanding that we need to WAKE UP and interact with our lives more intentionally than previously.

Many of us view unexpected negative events that happen in our lives as God's 'fault'. We struggle with anger towards God, thinking that He caused bad things to take place. But what the enemy intended for our destruction, God can always use for good. Maybe God allows things to happen to us because He is outside of time and can see the bigger picture. Maybe we needed a wake-up call, and the pain along the way is worth it for the impact of having a fully alive partner in the Kingdom.

Once we understand the sense of God's urgency, there comes a reckless abandon. We find a sureness and a peace that we know that we trust God. He has woken something inside us and it's now on Him to see it through. Suddenly that surrender comes more easily and the worry we may have had, fades away.

We shouldn't underestimate the timing of this sudden wake up call. Often God will have been trying to wake us up gently by bringing people, circumstances, speakers, books and all manner of things around us to try and rouse us. But if we miss it He may use something more drastic, because He doesn't want us missing His best for us. He has more life for us to live, but we have to engage with it more intentionally. We don't accidentally stumble upon His purposes. We have to seek His face, and intentionally commune with Him throughout each day.

Today, take stock of all that has happened in your life. Maybe you're in the midst of a major upheaval; take it as a compliment! It means God's not done - He sees that you can be more! Take time today to seek Him for HIS purpose in your circumstances.

Day 6

Alive in a new way

The thief comes only to steal and kill and destroy;
I have come that they may have life, and have it to the
full.
John 10:10

You make known to me the path of life;
you will fill me with joy in your presence,
with eternal pleasures at your right hand.
Psalm 16:11

When we are fully awake, it is like we are suddenly switched on to the creator and His masterpieces. There is a new zeal in life, an energy and excitement at what we can achieve each day as we walk with Him. Suddenly we find we can breathe. We have a supernatural peace and ability to rest which we didn't have before, and we find ourselves seeing people differently, like we're seeing them through His eyes. We interact with the day differently, understanding that He is always present, and there is always a lesson to be learned or a gift to be received from Him, or a blessing to be given to someone in partnership with Him.

This sometimes goes against how we 'feel', but when we wake up we find that we aren't defeated by circumstances as we may have been before. Instead we have a source of solutions and grace for what we're walking through. It's not because we're more confident in ourselves, but because we know we're linking arms with the maker and designer, the One whose idea this all was. He promises a life of fullness, but how often do we actually 'cash in' on this promise?

We often allow our days to be dictated by emotions, and let disappointments and struggles define our daily lives. But remaining alive in the spirit and awake to who we are in HIM enables us to overcome those things. This isn't the same as being 'on a high', which always ends with a crash. When we are fully awake and alive, we have a quiet consistency that isn't dependent on feelings. The circumstances and emotions of the day will pass tomorrow and be forgotten. It is the treasure from on high, sown into our hearts, that will remain forever. This is what feeds a fully awakened life.

Today, try to consciously identify what is determining the day's mood. Are you entirely manipulated by emotions and reactions to what is going on around you? Or are you able to remain alive and awake in the spirit, choosing joy, and keeping a quiet and constant heart, despite any hardships or struggle you might encounter? Find a way to be in His presence, and feast on the fullness of joy that He has promised you.

Day 7

Refreshment

He makes me lie down in green pastures,
he leads me beside quiet waters,
he refreshes my soul.
He guides me along the right paths
for his name's sake.
Psalm 23:2-3

Have you ever considered the sheep's role in this Psalm? No matter how good the shepherd, a sheep must leave the safety of the pen and step out to follow if it is to be led to a place of refreshment & rest. Like sheep, we, too, must share in the responsibility for our own refreshment.

As we said yesterday, it is natural to allow our feelings to dictate how our day goes. We can fall into the habit of sitting and waiting for God to refresh us, all the while allowing our feelings to sow seeds of bitter untruth into our hearts.

The process of refreshment starts with the act of believing God's spoken truth. When we are spiritually awake, our senses start to see God at work in every moment. We see people and situations as He sees them, and we begin to understand how He works in the unseen. Our inner spirit is awakened to its original design, and we begin to operate differently from before. The truth of today's verse becomes our reality, and we find refreshment by those still waters. Our soul can be restored, and we start to really believe that He will protect us.

But this doesn't mean we stop being human! We are all made with feelings and emotions, but part of our call to live disciplined lives means being masters over these. When we succeed at this, we will find it becomes natural to stand on truth rather than emotion. We find that the levels of refreshment are vastly raised. When we build our lives on an immovable truth, this becomes a solid rock under our feet, undergirding our decisions. Then we are operating as we were always intended to operate – in connection and conjunction with our maker, representing God's image.

Decide today to start the process of moving away from the sinking sands of feelings that dictate your day. Begin to climb up on the rock of truth, making it the basis for your day - your decisions, your choices, your identity and your family. Then true refreshment can begin.

Day 8

Drink from the source

Jesus answered, "Everyone who drinks this water will be thirsty again, 14 but whoever drinks the water I give them will never thirst. Indeed, the water I give them will become in them a spring of water welling up to eternal life."
John 4:13-14

So often, we wake up with our day defined by notifications that have arrived overnight, or emotions that surface when we open our eyes. We turn and look at our phones or worry about the school run. We remember stress or sadness or frustrations from the day before. But these are not what we should base our day on. They are passing, temporal, and designed by the enemy to take our attention away from where it should rest.

Once we have been awakened, things change. Our inner being rises up and everything in us longs to connect to our original source, our creator. We were made to commune with Him, as in the Garden of Eden. We wake up with a new approach to the day, with a thirst like someone who's traveled the desert, parched and desperate for a drink from the Source. Rather than letting the number of likes, emails or re-tweets define our mood, we have a determination to equip ourselves, connect, fill up, and position ourselves on truth.

Drink from the source

What if we woke up each day with a determination that reflects what is really going on around us? The scriptures are clear that we do not battle earthly flesh and blood; the battle is in the spiritual realm. This is where our daily fight should begin. This is the sphere in which we are destined to spend eternity, so it makes sense that we should be familiarizing ourselves with it. It is our spirit that will spend eternity with the King of Kings, not our mortal bodies. There are no Instagram notifications in Heaven!

I am all for social media and technology. All these things can be used for good, for the advancement of the Kingdom - for many of us, technology is how we use our gifts! However, the key is where we are finding our refreshment, our feeding, and our identity. If we are dependent on a post doing well, or emails arriving, or promotions, pay rises or our bosses approval, then we have missed the point.

Today, decide to discipline yourself to commit to turning to the Source first. Turn from the worldly things that can so easily distract us, and let the creator of the world fill you up.

If you think it is an issue that needs addressing, maybe start being more intentional about tracking the time you spend on social media, or whatever else it is that you may have replaced the source with.

Day 9

Shift in posture

For who is God besides the Lord?
And who is the Rock except our God?
It is God who arms me with strength
and keeps my way secure.
He makes my feet like the feet of a deer;
he causes me to stand on the heights.
He trains my hands for battle;
my arms can bend a bow of bronze.
Psalm 18:31-34

When we are awakened, everything about us changes – our stance and our outlook. The position of our heart changes and our spiritual posture shifts.

Imagine a person trying to go against the flow during London's rush hour. Imagine getting tossed about, carried by the flow of people all pushing to get onto the tube. This is a good analogy for our sleepy state. We may try and walk the opposite direction, but we're not really strong enough or alert enough to get past. We just get jostled and shoved in the direction of the majority.

So many of us are in this position. Our voices are stifled by the growing volume of the world - sometimes even the church. We are quick to betray our authenticity in order to conform to the box we're surrounded by. If we have our voices and strength sapped from us often enough, so many of us end up allowing our uniqueness to be extinguished, and we become just another shade of grey, amidst the thousands of others out there.

But when we are awakened, a warrior suddenly rises up in us. Our position becomes more intentional; our feet are poised for holding ground. We are not easily swayed, but alert, not allowing ourselves to be moved by oncoming traffic and pressures. Our voice suddenly becomes highly valuable, and we learn that while we may need to craft how we communicate, our authentic voice, is one of our gifts. We are a unique creation, and represent a unique facet of God's image that no one else on earth displays.

With this heightened awareness of attack, God's Spirit in us opens our eyes to the activity that goes on in the unseen, making us able to prepare for attacks and pressures before they arrive. This gives us an opportunity to use God's full armor (Eph 6), and hold our ground.

Take some time today to realign your posture. Maybe there is an area in your life that you've been 'sleepy' in, where you need to adopt a new posture for battle. Set aside time to ask God which piece of armor you need to make that change.

Day 10

New ground

Joshua told the people, "Consecrate yourselves, for tomorrow the Lord will do amazing things among you." Joshua said to the priests, "Take up the ark of the covenant and pass on ahead of the people." So they took it up and went ahead of them.
Joshua 3:5-6

Taking new ground is something that can appear scary to us. We look at our lives and think that we have been through so much and haven't go the energy to move forwards any more.

When we are awakened, we start to see how the seasons we've walked through, the tests, the fires and the trials that we've faced, are all part of our training. Those smaller valleys and hills we've endured were preparation for the mountains and gorges that God wants us to take for His kingdom.

When Joshua took Jericho, he didn't do it from a command center, through comms, with other people's boots on the ground. In the same way, we cannot conquer ground we haven't walked. Walking through things is what enables us to conquer them - but not only that, it gives us the ability to navigate others through the land mines and dangers of that land.

In the kingdom of God, nothing is wasted, and nothing is selfish. When we have put on the armor of God and stood our ground, it's sometimes the right thing to turn around and see how far He's brought us. We realize that the hill we've just conquered wasn't Mount Everest after all, but that what we've learned along the way will help us on our next quest.

Sometimes there may even be people behind us who need a helping hand with exactly the thing we've just been through.

Stepping out and taking new ground requires obedience, determination, persistence in prayer, and a grit to be able to stick to what we've heard God say. Joshua didn't waver in his battle plan of marching around Jericho seven times. Not a single arrow was fired, or sword wielded, not even a shout was heard. They obeyed, they were determined, and they silently and persistently prayed as they walked.

What is your Jericho? And what is the battle plan that God has given you? It may not be conventional! Take time today to ask God for clear vision and strategy, and make a commitment to walk the ground you're wanting to conquer. This may mean going on a prayer walk, or it may mean using the experiences you've already walked through to help others, but whatever the case, taking new ground requires courage. Ask God today for all you need to conquer the new ground He's giving you.

DAY 11

New perspective

The word of the Lord came to me: "What do you see, Jeremiah?" "I see the branch of an almond tree," I replied.
Jeremiah 1:11

For this is the reason the gospel was preached even to those who are now dead, so that they might be judged according to human standards in regard to the body, but live according to God in regard to the spirit.
1 Peter 4:6

With a new posture and approach to the day comes a new understanding of both our calling and our role in the Kingdom of God.

Seeing the world through spiritual eyes brings a new perspective on everything. We gain greater understanding of what is going on 'behind the scenes', because we are partnering with God on a spiritual level.

This new perspective allows us to understand how to pray, stand, and really engage with our days in a way that facilitates the advancement of Kingdom of God in our lives and the lives of those around us.

NEW PERSPECTIVE

So often we are afraid of what we might see. We shy away from seeing this world because we know that dealing with it is going to require exercising some spiritual muscles. We would rather remain asleep and dozy, and be carried by the crowds. It's easier. It's more convenient. But it's not what God requires.

God has left exercise a choice. Just as going to the gym is an option that many don't take up, so is spiritual exercise. Our inner spirit not only needs waking up, it needs exercising. We must familiarize ourselves with operating in this realm and practice hearing, seeing, and standing.

Today, make time to ask "what do you see?". Ask God what His take on a specific person or situation is, and let Him show you. You might be surprised what you discover.

If you're walking through a desert season, take heart! He has brought you here to meet with you, to speak tenderly to you, and to do a new thing. Thank him for the season you're in, and position your heart to be ready for the new thing that is coming!

DAY 12

Awakened to our senses

*Then Ananias went to the house and entered it.
Placing his hands on Saul, he said, "Brother Saul,
the Lord—Jesus, who appeared to you on the road
as you were coming here—has sent me so that you
may see again and be filled with the Holy Spirit."
Immediately, something like scales fell from Saul's
eyes, and he could see again. He got up and was
baptized, and after taking some food, he regained his
strength.
Acts 9:17-19*

We have all heard of stories of people who've encountered a near death experience. Suddenly everything is alive and more vibrant to them, they notice the smells, the sounds, the sights around them more than they ever had before.

What if this is exactly what happens to us spiritually? What if we've been so asleep to all that is around us that we have lost our sense of spiritual smell, and spiritual insight into what is occurring around us.

Imagine that sudden deep breath that someone takes after being unconscious. This is what it is like to be truly awakened.

Having been 'out for the count' and unengaged for so long, we suddenly take that long, deep breath of the Spirit. We become aware of the smell in the room, the taste in our mouth, and the feel of things around us in a way we may not have noticed before.

Our discernment of what is around us is suddenly intensified. This is a gift that will dull if we do not actively stay in this place of heightened sensitivity. It's an intentional position that, with practice and prayer, we can remain in.

Warning: staying in a place of heightened sensitivity comes with its risks. We are more vulnerable to attack. We are a softer clay in the potter's hands, which is where we should be. Being more sensitive can mean that things hurt more, but this can be a good thing: we are in a place where we are not compromising, nor having our senses dulled and hardened. We are right where we need to be.

Take time today to intentionally position yourself to take that deep breath of the spirit. Ask Him to breathe life into you so that you can sense what is really going on around you. Ask Him to reveal to you the smells, tastes and 'feel' for things around you during the day. Watch a new understanding of the world around you unravel!

Day 13

Our allegiance

No one can serve two masters. Either you will hate the one and love the other, or you will be devoted to the one and despise the other. You cannot serve both God and money.
Luke 16:13

In the story of Hezekiah found in 2 Kings, we are confronted with the protagonist Uriah - the high priest. Uriah didn't fulfil his priestly duties faithfully - it says in 2 Kings 16:16 that he "did just as king Ahaz had ordered".

This priest was not in awe of the presence of the God he got to tend to and serve daily. He did not have 'the fear of the Lord'. Rather, he was more concerned with keeping his master happy. Uriah served his king, not his God. He saw no problem with replacing the altar of the Lord in the temple with a foreign altar. He saw no problem with stripping the temple of its wealth and beauty in order to appease Israel's enemies. He saw no problem with taking part in child sacrifice at the order of the king.

1Peter 2:9 says we are a Royal Priesthood and the temple of the Holy Spirit. We are called to tend to the presence of God in our lives, and to spend time in the Holy place - much like Uriah.

But as Luke says in today's verse, Luke 16:13, we cannot serve two masters. Uriah embodies the severity of compromise – he ended up facilitating an entire nation in idolatry. Compromise always leads to idolatry.

Once we are fully awakened to whom we are serving, it suddenly becomes apparent just how much compromise we make during the day. This is when we can start making adjustments and changes that help us to be a priest that serves just one master; the correct King.

During the day today, take some time to really analyze which master you're serving in the things you're doing. If you need to make adjustments, maybe start journaling one area at a time in which you'd like to see changes occur.

DAY 14

Our destiny

Commit your way to the Lord;
trust in him and he will do this:
He will make your righteous reward shine like the
dawn,
your vindication like the noonday sun.

Be still before the Lord
and wait patiently for him;

do not fret when people succeed in their ways,
when they carry out their wicked schemes.
Psalm 37:5-7

Even when he was tending sheep and slaying bears, David was destined to be king. He wasn't awakened to his full purpose yet, but he was surrendered to God's will and plan for his life, even when he was not included when his seven brothers met with King Saul. Not one moment of his sheep tending days were wasted. God didn't ignore him until He needed David to step into being King; He carefully crafted his time on the hillside to prepare him for what was coming.

Having been anointed as the future King, David may have spent time wondering why his life didn't look that different. One minute he's chosen from all his brothers to be the next

King of all Israel, the next he's back on the hillside with those pesky sheep! Nothing changed - no grandeur, no palace, no servants, no wine, women or frivolities. Just sheep.

Sometimes this is what happens to us. We are given a glimpse of what our destiny might be, maybe through dreams we've had, words we've been given or the desires of our hearts. Then we have to wait!

But take courage - this process of waiting is an opportunity for us to wake up, so as to be ready for our destiny and to understand what our identity really is. It is a place and space for us to become secure and at peace with what is coming before it arrives. That makes us far more steady so that we can become stable vessels for God to use when it's time to do what we were made for.

Take some time today to journal what you feel your call and destiny might be, and think about how what you're walking through could be preparing you and really awakening you to what God has planned for you.

DAY 15

Our gifts

...for God's gifts and his call are irrevocable.
Romans 11:29

Each person is created uniquely with their own gifts, talents, dreams and calling. If we fall asleep to this, those gifts may never be used for their original intention.
- Day 3

The gifts, calls and destiny are irrevocable. God doesn't change His mind. They were decided before the foundation of the earth and His plans for our lives do not waiver. However, we have to choose to engage with them. They're there for the taking, if we follow His lead.

But these gifts and calling aren't there to make us great or to give us a bigger or better life; they're there to glorify Him and to further His kingdom. We can often add expectations or conditions to the call of God and expect to receive something in return for stepping out or engaging with what He has in store for us. But that's not how it works!

As we trust and honor God with our lives, so He trusts and blesses us. But this only happens when we arrive at a place where we are willing to step into our destiny without expecting anything in return. The principle of heaven is that blessings are poured out on us - whether in this life or in eternity. But it cannot be the motive for our obedience! Keeping a pure heart towards our motives is something that we all have to grapple with, and it always comes back to a very simple and basic principle: if we aren't content with our efforts and gifts being only for an audience of One, then we aren't ready for an audience at all.

Today is really about making a decision as to whether we're willing to engage with God's plan, without conditions or expectations. The only thing we need to know is that God is good, and His plans are for us are for our benefit.

But we need to remember - if we engage and activate His gifts and calls, we become a target for the enemy. We are like soldiers moving from reserve to being on active duty. We must make our decisions fully understanding that the enemy wants us to stay asleep to our potential, unaware of our role in the Kingdom and partnership with God.

Today comes with a message that is sometimes a hard pill to swallow. Take some time to see if you've attached conditions to your gifts. Is there an agenda or expectation that you're subconsciously holding God to before being willing to set out in your gifts? This exercise requires honesty and deep heart searching.

Day 16

Awakened to others

By this everyone will know that you are my disciples,
if you love one another.
John 13:35

When we intentionally 'switch on' to God and His plans, we allow Him to fill us, making us a vessel that carries the presence of God everywhere we go. As we allow the renewing of our mind to occur by receiving the mind of Messiah, we will start to see our hearts and desires change to match His.

God is love, and when He took on the form of man, He had a servant heart. As we walk through this awakening transformation, we will start to notice that we have more love and compassion for those around us. As we observe the world around us, we see those we cross paths with through a different lens. We have a transformed heart, which gives us a different perspective. Often in life we approach others with an unintentionally selfish outlook. We are defensive, and well trained to look at what's in it for us, meaning we often assume the worst of others.

Something that often makes people look twice at believers is when they serve or love others without expecting anything in return. It's a love without agenda. A compassion without conditions. A serving without needing repayment.

Operating like this is not a cultural norm, and seeing it can confuse people. But when this awakening happens, it's one of the most exciting and liberating things that can occur in our lives. We often realize just how much of our own worth we were looking for in loving and serving others.

But we should find our identity entirely in His love for us, not at the expense of others. When we start to get a glimpse of how He feels about others, it becomes so much easier to love without conditions; we can act without an agenda when we don't expect anything in return!

Try to be conscious today about noting the conditions you may be putting on your love for others. Start to serve just to serve, and love just because. Choose joy, even when others don't notice or are ungrateful.

Day 17

Illuminate

The eye is the lamp of the body. If your eyes are healthy, your whole body will be full of light. But if your eyes are unhealthy, your whole body will be full of darkness. If then the light within you is darkness, how great is that darkness!
Matthew 6:22-23

Waking up to a dark house is never fun; throwing open the drapes or the shutters floods the room with light and suddenly we see things as they truly are. We see the areas that need ordering, where there are piles of unsorted items. We spot the layers of dust and where the shadows still fall.

This is a great picture of what happens in our hearts when we are truly awakened to God and who we are in Him. When we fling open the blinds in our hearts and are saturated with His light, we suddenly see things differently. We don't realize how much we can't see until we add light. This is when I have found myself praying the prayer 'flood my heart in every part', and it's so important. We need to see the areas of our own hearts that are still dark and full of shadows, so that we can intentionally expose them to His light.

The principles of God's kingdom are always contrary to the principles of the world. The world is full of shadows and falsities, like when we think there is a monster in the room but it's just a morning robe hanging on the back of the door. When the light pours in and we see things as they really are, we realize that there is nothing to be afraid of with God on our side.

In the Kingdom of God, light always exposes. It may expose things that we need to rectify once we see them for what they are. It may expose parts of ourselves which we didn't know were there; idols which we hadn't realized had taken residence in our hearts, taking all our attention away from the true King.

Spend time today looking into the rooms of your heart and throwing open the drapes. You might be surprised what you find there! You may discover that your heart is more of a store room or attic than you thought, with old flames and sentimental junk being stored every where. Maybe it's time to clear some of those boxes out, so that your heart is clear and ordered, ready to be flooded by His light.

Day 18

His light in you

You are the light of the world. A town built on a hill cannot be hidden. Neither do people light a lamp and put it under a bowl. Instead they put it on its stand, and it gives light to everyone in the house. In the same way, let your light shine before others, that they may see your good deeds and glorify your Father in heaven.
Matthew 5:14-16

I live in Israel, near to the northern city of Haifa. Haifa is a very striking city because it is all built upon the mountain tops of the Mount Carmel range. As you approach Haifa, you drive along the flat, sea side highway, with the ocean on your left and the mountain tops on the right. At night, this scene is particularly striking, as the city is so illuminated - it's an incredible site to see a city, up high. It's certainly impossible to miss.

The verse for today is all about this. When we begin to operate as a 'fully awake' person, the light that fills us shines out, piercing through the darkness around us. Sometimes we are so afraid of the darkness that we forget that it just shows off the light. A candle in a room that is flooded with light doesn't have much impact. But a candle in pitch darkness looks exceptional and makes a striking impression, drawing people towards it.

Sometimes the light we start to emit when we're fully alive becomes a beacon of hope. It highlights the principles of God and the work of the Spirit, like a torch lighting the way. The beauty that God can bring about from the ashes is shown off by the illumination of Him in us. The darkness that surrounds us just shows off the light even more.

Our constant prayer should be that God shines His light on us, that His Light would flood our every part, every corner of our hearts. It's so easy for darkness to creep in when our light dims, or when we don't regularly kindle the embers of our fire. It's not that we have invited darkness into our lives, it's simply the absence of light. We must keep our fire fanned constantly, blazing bright, never letting the darkness have a chance. We must take responsibility for feeding our own fire.

Never underestimate the power that a light has. It can be a rescuing beacon in the middle of a storm for someone else. Take time today to analyze how your light is doing. Have you hidden it? Are you like a city on a hill that can't be missed? Make a commitment today to change what needs to change in order to allow your light shine bright.

Day 19

His voice

*Call to me and I will answer you and tell you great
and unsearchable things you do not know.
Jeremiah 3:33*

$\mathcal{I}$ think that the main point of being awakened in the first place is to arrive at a place where we truly hear the voice of God. It may not be an audible sound, but God is everywhere, desperately trying to communicate with the crown of His creation.

We have done a great job of restricting how we allow God to speak to us. Many of us expect for God to speak through a particular way of reading the bible, or through a very narrow genre of music which we have labeled 'worship'. But God isn't dictated by our constraints. He is bursting through our restrictions with explosions of love and communications, but if we're blinkered by our expectations, we risk missing it!

Being awakened to His voice isn't only about hearing Him more clearly but hearing Him in unlikely places. God is able to speak in the most unusual of situations. It shouldn't come as a great surprise when He speaks – we should always expect to hear His voice. He's constantly speaking, singing and praying over us, but we only tend to tune in to one kind of communication.

Often, because we are so wrapped up in circumstances we have been programmed to think of as 'bad', we miss God speaking. We put up walls and shields as a coping mechanism, and miss God shooting arrows of love and fresh air that could be seeing us through. This leads to feeling even more alone, deserted and abandoned.

We are created to communicate and dwell with God. When He calls out to us, we are designed to run to Him. Everything in us is created to respond to His voice; we are designed to walk with Him like the first humans did in Eden. All of creation is crying out in response to His creating voice, including us. All of us is responding to all of Him. And yet we often don't see that our cells are exploding with the life that He put there!

Today, ask God to remove the veil and the blinkers. Ask Him to allow you to fully wake up to His voice that is all around is you. He could be speaking through discipline, through a desert season, through provision, through loss, through success. Ask Him to soften your heart and to give in to the explosion of expression that there is in and around each one of us.

Day 20

His methods

*"For my thoughts are not your thoughts,
neither are your ways my ways,"
declares the Lord.*

*"As the heavens are higher than the earth,
so are my ways higher than your ways
and my thoughts than your thoughts."
Jeremiah 5:8-9*

Life is like an ocean. It's full of currents pulling us in directions we didn't know existed. It can get rough in an instant, but it can be beautiful and refreshing at times too. Sometimes we're ready and waiting for these waves, because we know we're walking through a storm. We saw them coming: it started with a light drizzle, the winds picked up, and we were ready with our coats, boots and umbrellas, heading as quickly as we can into calm waters.

Other times we're happily enjoying a quiet, peaceful picnic for the soul, and in an instant we are being pounded with the lashing rains of a storm that arrived with no warning. We're not ready! We're left outside in our summer clothes getting soaked to the bone, and our picnic has turned to a soggy, unappetizing mess. The rain stings our skin, and we can't see anything clearly, so we just sit there, getting drenched, hoping it'll pass quickly so we can get back to life.

But what if God had a plan in the suddenness of the storm? What if His intention is to catch us unawares? What if He didn't want picnic food to satisfy us anymore? What if He has things He wants to do in us during the storm? I'm certain that He wants us to stop fighting the tides and let Him carry us.

God knows that He gets a lot less done in us when we're prepared to fix all the things which are going 'wrong' around us. We don't look to see if these circumstances are God's way of doing a work in us, we just get on and 'fix' it. But perhaps that's exactly why some storms come suddenly out of the blue. Because in His mercy He saves us from ourselves, from our incessant need to 'fix' everything and find the easy way out.

God is always good. His grace abounds -it engulfs us, surrounds us, and carries us in His currents to the places He wants us to be. If we stop fighting the storm and all it brings, we might discover that we have been transformed, washed clean, renewed, restored and directed in ways we never could have accomplished for ourselves.

Today, try to remember that God isn't as interested in saving us from our circumstances, as He is in saving us from ourselves, using the circumstances as His tools. Follow Him into the eye of the storm, knowing that being in the storm with Him IS His great rescue plan.

DAY 21

His breath

Then the Lord God formed a man from the dust of the ground and breathed into his nostrils the breath of life, and the man became a living being.
Genesis 2:7

We all breathe. It's an involuntary action that we do whether we're awake or asleep, thinking about it or not, resting or running, happy or sad. Sometimes we are more aware of our breathing patterns than at other times, but we go through a large proportion of the day without thinking about our breathing.

I stopped to think recently about the meaning of this, and how often I consider the power of the breath of God. There are many scriptures that tell us about the power that the breath of God carries but to me, the breath of God is exemplified beautifully in the dandelion.

Imagine that I am this fragile plant, often viewed as a weed. I am not a beautiful towering rose bush, I am small and weak and easily trodden upon. But what happens when His breath is released upon me? Like dandelion seeds, I can suddenly fly!

At the right time, and in the right direction, I am released from all that has held me anchored and I'm flying, moving in a way I could never have moved myself. I am soaring, reaching heights and finding currents I didn't know existed, traveling to places that I've never seen.

And then what happens when I land after His breath has directed me? I multiply!

You see, the Kingdom of God isn't designed to be selfish. I may be blessed, I may receive gifts from God, but what is the point if I store it all up for myself? Instead we are being called to spread these seeds of love far and wide!

It all starts with the breath of God blowing upon us, freeing us, bringing us to life, and setting us up to multiply. It is a divine exchange that happens when He breathes upon us. Our gifts and dreams turn to color, and the hard parts of our hearts become alive. As we are sustained by His breath, He inspires us to pour out life and blessing to others, multiplying along the way. Without breath, we cannot live, speak, move or function.

Today, think about the areas in your life that God is starting to breathe on. Maybe there are gifts that you have already taken flight in and it's time for them to multiply. Or maybe there is a new gift that God is blowing upon you that you haven't realized needs to take flight! Make a conscious decision to allow God to blow upon your gifts and calling, and to not resist the direction He takes you in.

DAY 22

Fearless in failure

For the Spirit God gave us does not make us
timid, but gives us power, love and self-discipline.
2 Timothy 1:7

$\mathcal{I}$ love this quote from Pete Coggan about failure:

> *"You think you exist, but you don't. Millions of people*
> *believe in you, even get scared of your arrival. The idea of*
> *you has stunted some of the most ingenious and creative*
> *adventures this world has never seen. Give me the*
> *'pursuit in persistence', the beauty in trying and reaching,*
> *learning and speaking. The wonder in feedback and*
> *critique to reshape and grow deep."*

I agree with him that failure doesn't exist. The world has created this very scary monster called 'failure', that we think of as something that could jump out on us anytime. But I think it's really only a matter of how we view it. There are many ways we can condemn ourselves to failure in what we do because we've written our own version of what success is.

We've mentioned before that in the Kingdom of God, principles usually go contrary to those of the world, and that if we're not content with an audience of One, then we're not ready for an audience at all. So often we consider ourselves to have failed because we have measured ourselves against a worldly success monitor, rather than asking the simple question "Was it pleasing to His heart?". If the answer to that question is a 'yes', then we should be confident in our success.

Engaging with a spirit of failure can lead us to be shy and timid in our decision making. But failure is just a cheap, dressed up, counterfeit version of fear. It doesn't exist, and more to the point, 'God has not given us a spirit of fear, but of power, love and self-discipline.' Show me a person in history who has operated in power, love and self-discipline, and has failed - I doubt there is one. When we operate in God's spirit, failure and fear disappear.

Sometimes the threat of 'worldly' failure can give us a healthy persistence, but it shouldn't define who we are or be a label we ever add to anything we do. We should always be ready and willing to accept feedback and critique, but we must maintain confidence in the call of God, not letting the fear of what we see shake the faith in what we've heard.

Flipping this understanding of success and failure on its head should eradicate the fear of failure that so many of us live under. Once we understand that our affirmation comes from blessing His heart and turning every act into worship, there is no such thing as failure.

Take time today to identify the areas of your life where you may be worried about failure. Turn your fears into courage and ask to Spirit of God to give you power, love and self-discipline in this area. A phrase I find myself saying to encourage myself is, "I will not allow the fear of what I see shake the faith in what I've heard".

Day 23

Fierce

Awake, awake, Zion,
clothe yourself with strength!
Put on your garments of splendor,
Jerusalem, the holy city.
The uncircumcised and defiled
will not enter you again.

Shake off your dust;
rise up, sit enthroned, Jerusalem.
Free yourself from the chains on your neck,
Daughter Zion, now a captive.
Isaiah 52:1-2

Since we've established that failure doesn't exist, we know we don't need to fear it. We may get knocked down, or fall, but we have to learn that this isn't a bad thing! We will learn a new tactic or a new strategy with every knock and fall, and become stronger because of it. Our scars become the map of our testimony, not to be despised or regretted, but to be celebrated, because they represent wisdom gained and lessons learned.

Like we said on day 10, we cannot conquer new ground if we do not walk on it. We cannot take new ground by sitting on the sidelines watching others advance. We must be on the front lines, taking the steps ourselves. That involves MOVING! It involves stepping out, being brave and finding the fierceness we have inside.

One thing we might associate the with word 'fierce' is a Lion - and that would be absolutely right! Lions can be fierce, and yet God, who we know is gentle, loving and kind, calls Himself 'The Lion of the tribe of Judah'. Fierce doesn't need to mean destructive or aggressive. I believe that being fierce means being tenacious, standing our ground, no matter how much the world may tell us that what we're doing doesn't make sense. Read the verse from today - this isn't a gentle lullaby, this is a call to action! It's about getting up and adorning ourselves with strength!

Sometimes we pray for God to do these things for us, but often the answer lies in us making a decision for ourselves. In today's verse God is requiring Jerusalem to do these things for herself! "Put on your strength!"; "Loosen yourself from the bonds around your neck!"; "Shake yourself from the dust and RISE UP!" There is a clear call to action that results in a fierce, fearless, tenacious stance.

Today is about resolving to move forward. We are all in a battle, and if we don't move forwards we will end up regressing. It may not take any physical steps; it may just be a mental shift, or a spiritual acknowledgment. It may be a major change or a new chapter, but whatever it is, resolve to lower your chin, dig your heels in, and take that ground. You've got this! Find your fierce!

Day 24

Quiet and loud

*The Lord said, "Go out and stand on the mountain in
the presence of the Lord, for the Lord is about to
pass by." Then a great and powerful wind tore the
mountains apart and shattered the rocks before
the Lord, but the Lord was not in the wind. After
the wind there was an earthquake, but the Lord was
not in the earthquake. After the earthquake came a
fire, but the Lord was not in the fire. And after the
fire came a gentle whisper. When Elijah heard it, he
pulled his cloak over his face and went out and stood
at the mouth of the cave.*
1 Kings 19:11-13

Have you ever stopped to notice the things around us
that have the 'loudest voice'? I've often noticed that it's the
unspoken things, the words that aren't uttered, that seem to
speak the loudest. So often we find that body language and
facial expressions say more than any word, shout, or scream!

Sometimes we think that the way to get our voice heard
is to shout louder - to have more view, more friends, more
followers, or tweets. But God wasn't found in the earth-
shattering earthquake, or the ravaging, landscape-changing

fire. He wasn't found in the monumental, rearranging whirlwind. He was found in the life-transforming whisper.

And yet somehow we always find ourselves craving that which is loud! We so easily slip into finding our value in the wrong places, and forget the impact of a loving God, whose word is truth. We pump more and more noise into our souls all day, then wonder why we aren't refreshed! We need to switch the noise off, quieten our spirits and put ourselves in a position to hear His whisper. That's what our souls are created to yearn for.

God's whisper is louder than anything else, because it has the greatest impact. It leaves change in its wake, transformation after just a breath. When thinking about the impact that we leave, we need to change our perspective. We need to think more about the impact of Kingdom and Spirit. We aren't going to be able to make a dent on the vast number of Tweets each day or the billions of videos that appear on YouTube. Instead, let us focus on aligning ourselves with the will of God in our lives, trusting and resting in the fact that He will breath on us in His time. His breath will bring the impact, not ours. His whisper through a willing vessel will cut through the noise to those who are inclined to hear. Being in the center of His will is the most impacting and powerful position any human can be in.

Today take some time to think about areas of your life where you might be trying to shout in your own strength. Maybe you're filling your life with noise and you need to switch off. Maybe it's time to let go and allow God to whisper through you. His whisper is always going to be louder than our biggest noise.

Day 25

Weak and brave

But he said to me, "My grace is sufficient for you, for my power is made perfect in weakness." Therefore I will boast all the more gladly about my weaknesses, so that Christ's power may rest on me.
2 Corinthians 12:9

There are so many examples through scripture of 'unlikely' heroes, the outcasts of society who were marginalized and passed over. The prostitutes and lepers, the orphans and the widows, those that culture said were done and should be forgotten. And yet, these were the ones that Yeshua chose to hang out with.

We may not have any of these labels ourselves, but we might feel like we will never amount to much, or that we are a little pathetic, or weak. It can be easy to feel like we are not worthy enough to do anything of consequence and we'd be better left in the shadows. In some ways I think it can be a gift when people feel this way, because then we don't have to walk through a season of being humbled. Yeshua uses those who have already been brought 'down' to that place.

When it comes to partnering with God, we just need to be brave. He can work with a weak person, because He is strong. He can call a forgotten person, because He doesn't forget any part of His creation. God can partner with a humble person, because their ego won't try and take credit for God's work. All we need to do is be brave enough to take His hand.

Once we start seeing our weaknesses as opportunities for God to work with, we can become brave and willing vessels who won't get in God's way. He likes to be glorified through us, and when we operate out of a place of strength, some of the glory goes to us. This isn't to say that we shouldn't exercise 'strengths' in giftings - we should always do our best! But we shouldn't use our own muscle power to get those giftings 'used' by God.

Take some time today to celebrate the weaknesses of which you've been critical. He will make up for all that you think you're missing, because that's how it works best anyway. What you will often discover, when you grab that hand, is that God knew what He was doing all along, and that He'd made you with exactly the ingredients needed for the task He's inviting you to join Him in.

Day 26

Small and strong

David said to the Philistine, "You come against me
with sword and spear and javelin, but I come against
you in the name of the Lord Almighty, the God of
the armies of Israel, whom you have defied. This day
the Lord will deliver you into my hands…"

1 Samuel 17:45-46a

My attention has recently been drawn to David and his confrontation with Goliath. Many of us will know this story - some of us have heard this story since we were small. We've grown up having David a hero to us, loving the image of a shepherd boy defeating a skilled, warrior giant!

And yet, there are elements of this story that we could really apply to our own lives that sometimes get overlooked. Firstly, David was weak, probably only teen or pre-teen, and on cheese delivery duty! He wasn't intending to go and fight a giant on this particular errand. He was just being a dutiful son, delivering lunch to his brothers. The fact that he saw the opportunity to fight really shows the extent of David's courage.

We may look at ourselves and see a small, weak, pre-teen version of a spiritual warrior. Certainly, I have fallen prey to these thoughts. We think we are too small to take on the giants that we see, and that we don't have the tools or experience to take them down. So we sit at the back of the camp and quake in fear, hoping the giant doesn't notice us and passes us by. We choose NOT to engage.

But David chose to get in there with just a sling and five pebbles. To me, these pebbles represent of our gifts. When they are left to themselves, they are just rough, colorless, stones in a collection of many. They're not anything special. But when our gifts are dusted with the fingerprints of the One who put them there, these pebbles suddenly become something unique, something powerful, something that can be used in a way that no one would have thought of.

So - what if we chose to engage with the giants, and stop viewing ourselves as too small? What if we decided to use the 'pebbles' that God has deposited in us? What if we let Him direct those pebbles as we pick them up, using the courage that He puts in us? Who knows what giants we will slay! The key is to focus on how strong God is, not how strong the giant is!

Take time today to identity what your pebbles might be, and commit to stopping belittling yourself – with God, you and your gifts can slay giants!

Day 27

Fully alive

You will go out in joy
and be led forth in peace;

the mountains and hill
will burst into song before you,

and all the trees of the field
will clap their hands.'
Isaiah 55:12

"'I tell you," he replied, "if they keep quiet, the stones
will cry out."
Luke 19:40

When we allow God's breath to fill our lungs and His light to flood our heart, not only do we see the dusty corners, the shadows and the unexpected items cluttering up our hearts, We also become fully alive. We've always been alive, we've breathed every day of our lives, we've functioned as much as we've been able throughout life. But what if we haven't?

What if there is a whole way of living that we've never experienced? We've been alive, but not fully. Many go through life like the walking dead going through the motions, but don't notice that we've not breathed in deep for a while. We've not noticed a clear sky, or been refreshed by the dew beneath our feet. Maybe we haven't ever stopped to notice the trees swaying, dancing to give Him glory, or the sunlight dancing on the surf at the beach, which can touch us to our core.

When we stop, and breathe Him in deep, we will start to realize that every atom that He has created in us is bursting with His life in us, in expression of who He is. It may be that we express this in different ways, Not everyone expresses their creator in the same creative way, it may be in relationship, business or sports, but it's not about WHAT we do, it's the fact that we are a creation, and all creation is crying out in worship of Him, including the very atoms that we're made up of.

We often lose sight of the fact that all of creation, and our very bodies are made to reflect Him and show off His handiwork. It's all crying out in response to Him and sometimes we just need to stop and notice! Wouldn't it be a shame if one day we find out that the rocks around us were crying out because we had forgotten to worship?

Take some time today to intentionally look around yourself, find the beauty in what's around you, join with creation in an expression of worship. This is the place when we are most fully alive.

Day 28

Dare to fall

After two days he will revive us;
on the third day he will restore us,
that we may live in his presence.

Let us acknowledge the Lord;
let us press on to acknowledge him.

As surely as the sun rises,
he will appear;

he will come to us like the winter rains,
like the spring rains that water the earth.
Hosea 6:2-3

"The bird who dares to fall is the bird who learns to fly" is a famous, seemingly anonymous quote which packs a punch! Birds often learn to fly by being kicked out of the nest by their parents. Sometimes they are even allowed to just free fall, with the parent swooping under them at the last minute to save them from plunging to the ground. Eagles are commonly known to practice this technique with their young. The eaglet is repeatedly pushed out of the nest and falls, flapping desperately until their parent catches them on their wings and takes them back up to the nest. This is repeated over and over as the eaglet's desperate flapping becomes more and more intentional and effective, until suddenly, they're flying!

Dare to fall

The point is though, that in order for that bird to learn to fly, they must dare to fall. They must take the risk and step into the unknown to try in the first place. That stomach churning moment when we step off the edge of an abseiling wall, or jump from a plane, or stand on a stage to sing for the first time, is the moment we need to learn to embrace! It represents taking new ground, advancing in our gifts, and stepping into a new season.

We can get so attached to our nests - or to the easy comfort of our sofas - that we don't want to step out onto the mountain side that awaits us. We are quite happy to veg out and watch TV, not realizing that as we do, our muscles and 'wings' are not developing as they should. The longer we go without stepping out, the less effective our wings will be when we eventually decide that maybe we should be flying, doing what we were created for, since we are, after all, a bird!

There are promises in the Bible to encourage us to take risks. Today's verse promises that He will restore us so that we may live in His presence. He also promises that as surely as the sun rises, He will appear, and come to us like winter rains. There is no down side to these promises,

Make a list today of small ways you can start to step out of your nest. It may be something as small as adjusting a bad habit, or something larger, like applying for a new course! Whatever it is, and wherever you're at, there is always something we can do to be intentional about moving towards the edge of the nest.

Day 29

Taking the risk

*Now faith is confidence in what we hope for and
assurance about what we do not see.
Hebrews 11:1*

A bird doesn't have an identity crisis when standing at the edge of the nest. It may feel afraid to step into the unknown and do something new, but there are some truths in which it can always find security. There is no doubt that it has wings, and certainly no doubt whether or not it is a bird.

When God speaks to us about His will in our lives, we, too, can find security. We do not find it in ourselves, but in the truths we know about His identity and character. In God, we can be confident in what we hope for, and have assurance in what we do not see – that He will catch us if we fall. He will not let us plunge to our deaths!

When we decide to step out of the nest it is a risk. There may be a moment after we have stepped out in faith, when we feel like we're free falling! But He's right next to us, His eye is on us, and He will swoop in and save us when we need it, as long as that is His perfect will for our lives. This is where the phrase from day 22 is useful: "Do not let the fear of what you see, shake the faith in what you've heard"!

The important thing to remember is that we may have a very different perspective on exactly when we need to be saved. So many of us have felt abandoned by God, wondering why He hasn't yet swooped in and stopped our free fall. We can't understand why He has left us to plummet to an inevitable death. But God sees the size of the mountain far more accurately than we do. He shaped it and formed it, and He was the one who placed us there.

This is why we can be confident. God knows that one day we'll be jumping from our nests and learning to fly from the precipice. He can see the height. He knows when and where the shadows will be. He sees it all. We can be confident that when God has spoken, we can have hope in the future, and assurance in all that we've yet to see.

Today is about finding peace as we stand on that nest edge, choosing to believe in what God has spoken over us about our identity and value. That truth makes us surefooted, allowing us to stand firm. Ask God to give you peace about what He's saying to you, so you can find the courage to jump.

Day 30

Soar

Do you not know?
Have you not heard?

The Lord is the everlasting God,
the Creator of the ends of the earth.

He will not grow tired or weary,
and his understanding no one can fathom.

He gives strength to the weary
and increases the power of the weak.

Even youths grow tired and weary,
and young men stumble and fall;
but those who hope in the Lord
will renew their strength.

They will soar on wings like eagles;
they will run and not grow weary,
they will walk and not be faint.
Isaiah 40:28–30

What happens when that baby bird has been kicked out of the nest over and over again?

It starts to exercise its wings. It starts understanding what that part of its body is for. It starts practicing, strengthening, growing; it becomes intentional about how it uses that part of its anatomy. It begins to fly!

We are the same. When we realize that there's a part of us that we've not used before, we should practice it. Maybe it's prayer, or worship, or art, or counseling - it could be anything! We must strengthen that muscle and become intentional about our development, so that one day, when the time is right, we can catch that current, rise up on the wind, and truly soar.

That's when we know that our time in the desert, the season of 'falling', is coming to a close. God sends us currents to catch, which will take us higher and further than ever before. He gives us a bird's eye view on situations in our own or others' lives. In that moment, we see His perspective and receive His clarity in ways we haven't been able to before.

On this final day, take some time to figure out which season you're in. It may be that you're dreaming in one area of your life, that you're teetering on the edge of the nest wondering if you dare to fall in another area, and truly soaring in another! Take some time to commit to the next stage in each of these areas.

It's time to be fully awakened to all that God has made you to be. It's time to become fully alive in Him, partnering with Him in furthering His kingdom. It's time to catch the currents that He has ready for you.

It's time to soar!

Reviews of Dare to Ask

What you are about to read is like a good movie with various characters, vantage points and visceral moments that are all connected by a common theme – one of great risk and great reward. I think there is something in all of us that wants to believe for great things. *Dare to Ask*, explores that belief by reintroducing a cast of biblical characters whose experiences and decisions clearly correlate with life's challenges and circumstances today.

Like a master archaeologist, Simcha skillfully brushes away the dust and debris that has covered over dormant dreams so that divine destiny can be rediscovered once again – not just the destination, but the process. The revelation in the title chapter alone is well worth the price of admission, but the waves of wisdom, insight, honesty and personal application continue to roll until the very last page.

Dare to Ask challenges the resigned mindset that we are merely silent spectators in this life and beautifully reminds us that dreams are possible, miracles are real and hope is attainable if you just dare to ask.

Steve Carpenter
Founder, Highway 19 Ministries – Jerusalem

~

To the reader of *Dare to Ask*, I would say that when you reach the end of the book, you will conclude that this has been a kairos moment. It is a serendipity, a surprise discovery. Instead of it focusing on aspects of worship from a gifted worship leader, you will be taken on a moving personal journey that deepens your love for the Messiah. It leaves a lot of questions unanswered, but you are left with the deep assurance that the Lord is in control. As readers, we are simply left to keep on asking and keep on trusting. This is a beautiful devotional book written from the heart.

Dr David Elms
International Christian Embassy Jerusalem UK Director

~

Dare To Ask has a beautiful tapestry of practicality and spirituality woven throughout the pages. It challenges readers to dream our God-given dreams, use our God-given gifts, and remove clutter from our hearts so that we can experience the fullness of what God has for us. Through her testimony and scriptural insights, Simcha demonstrates how to be grateful in all things – including trials and desert places. If you need encouragement, restoration or a fresh stirring of hope in your heart, you will find it here! Prepare to go deeper...

Michael & Sara Thorsby
Burn 24-7 New Bern, NC Directors (USA)

Available Now
simchanatan.com

OUT NOW

SIMCHA NATAN

simchanatan.com/awakened-ep

Made in the USA
Columbia, SC
16 February 2019